UNDER THE ENEMY SKY

UNDER THE ENEMY SKY

Peter D. Webb

Copyright © 2020 Peter D. Webb

The moral right of the author has been asserted.

Apart from any fair dealing for the purposes of research or private study, or criticism or review, as permitted under the Copyright, Designs and Patents Act 1988, this publication may only be reproduced, stored or transmitted, in any form or by any means, with the prior permission in writing of the publishers, or in the case of reprographic reproduction in accordance with the terms of licences issued by the Copyright Licensing Agency. Enquiries concerning reproduction outside those terms should be sent to the publishers.

Matador
9 Priory Business Park,
Wistow Road, Kibworth Beauchamp,
Leicestershire. LE8 0RX
Tel: 0116 279 2299
Email: books@troubador.co.uk
Web: www.troubador.co.uk/matador
Twitter: @matadorbooks

ISBN 978 1838595 500
British Library Cataloguing in Publication Data.
A catalogue record for this book is available from the British Library.

Printed and bound in Great Britain by 4edge Limited
Typeset in 11pt Minion Pro by Troubador Publishing Ltd, Leicester, UK

Matador is an imprint of Troubador Publishing Ltd

To my grandchildren.
May they be able to live in a peaceful world.

Contents

Preface ix

1 Early Days 1
2 Battle of Britain 12
3 The Middle Years 20
4 The Night of the Doodlebug 34

Afterthoughts 61

Preface

A year or two back one of my grand-daughters was studying recent history at school and the course of her studies embraced the events of the Second World War. Classroom activities included an exhibition of collected wartime artefacts, and it was incumbent upon friends and relatives, familiar with the era, to see what they had inherited and what might be sitting in the loft. I was able to contribute a tin hat and a gas mask, both relics of the day and inherited from family activities of the time.

I was also asked to provide a brief account of my recollections of the period so that she might complete her studies with first hand information.

I realised that I was five years of age in 1939 and 11 years old when the conflict in Europe finally ended in 1945. I also had the 'benefit' of living in Croydon for most of the duration, which was a prime part of the war zone and where activity in the air was both incoming and outgoing. I might have a great deal more to recall than a brief sumary for the classroom on two sheets of paper.

I began to realise that memories of long-forgotten events were coming to the fore, and if my grand-daughter was writing an essay, I might be able to write a book.

In those early days, my original home town was near enough centre stage to some of the aerial action during the Battle of Britain and the dramatic events, in the follow-on years, above our heads and on the ground.

This war zone endured endless overflying by enemy raiders, attacking targets near and far, night and day, and was at the receiving end of attacks from V1 and V2 weapons during the latter stages of the war. It was also an era to witness the responding armadas of Allied bombers which flew over us on their retaliatory missions from bases far and wide inland, reaching out to targets in the Nazi heartland.

I set about writing this account in the following pages.

Chapter 1

Early Days

81 YEARS HAVE PASSED since September 1939 when Britain found it necessary to declare War against Hitler's Nazi Germany following his invasion of Poland, inaugurating the start of World War ll. Hitler had invaded several parts of Europe, beyond his own legitimate frontier, and the process was to continue with plans to occupy most of Europe and establish the empire of the Third Reich; Our Politicians had been bracing themselves for this inevitable development for some while especially as we knew that we were also on the waiting list for his potential colonization.

I had been under pressure, for some while, from Grandchildren, having reached this era in their studies of 20th Century history, and the historical events leading up to the

War, as the source of information, what better source than a Relative who had actually experienced an aspect of this considerable event, to finish off their classroom account.

This particular account deals with experiences that have been difficult to erase, continuously dramatic but also events dangerous and life threatening, occurring during the most formative period in a young person's life.

In July 1939, I was at the junior age of 5 years. In August of that year a summer holiday was arranged 'en famille' to the Norfolk coast, at the resort of Gorleston-on-Sea. Parents, elder brother, younger sister and an accompaniment of family friends, wives and husbands enjoying the surrogacy of Aunts and Uncles to the younger generations. My brother being 5 years ahead of me was getting to grips with the world. To me he knew everything, and my sister over two years my junior, the apple of the family's eye and at the very start of the learning stage. I suppose she had to endure a reputation for knowing very little. The beach and seashore held no bounds for her including kicking in my sand castles and making a brave attempt at her own. The sun was out most days and the summer beach held its own attractions to young and old alike.

We all stayed at a guest house a street or two back from the beach area. Breakfasts were a substantial affair in those days, arranged strictly between set times and usually inaugurated with the sound of a gong struck in the hallway of the building by an enthusiastic waiter. The dining room was crowded and meal tables set close together, our family was on one table etc. Guest holiday makers of the day were of a reserved disposition although with a style of informal dress indicating they were off to enjoy themselves, mainly on the beach as soon as the meal was over. Children were expected to behave themselves although looked over with affectionate smiles and kind words from fellow guests. Breakfast was always a three-course meal starting with porridge. Hot porridge was the universal hors d'ouvres to the first meal of the day in those days, even in high summer. Breakfast cereals had not really taken off yet and fruit juices were comparatively unknown.

When the porridge arrived my brother and I were fascinated by the fact that as you tipped the plate, the area of the plate beneath the porridge was perfectly clean. This went on until one morning I managed to tip the lot into my lap, which naturally caused a commotion, however I eventually fathered three children so I don't believe much long-term damage resulted in this mishap. After breakfast, we were ready for the beach.

I was beginning to learn that a War was imminent but not to understand any course of events or their implications. It was being mentioned a lot and I wondered what this event would be. One afternoon there was a lot of excitement on the beach as word got around that the Fleet was on the move and we would see it from the coast, out at sea. In modern day terms, it was to be a substantial Royal Navy task force, moving to destinations unknown, to action stations. We were on the threshold of War.

Sometime later, movements out to sea came into view, binoculars were produced, my father and uncle stood at the water's edge and busily studied the horizon, their shirts billowing in the on-shore summer breeze. My father holding the 'glasses' leaned forward as if expecting to get a better view. The beach was filled with animated conversation as levels of excitement grew. Binoculars were a regular and fashionable accompaniment to holidays and recreational events in those days, as with box cameras, they were the 'in thing' to have on the beach; in the same way, today, that we cherish a mobile phone, I-pad and snorkel in similar circumstances.

The binoculars were handed backwards and forwards eventually reaching my brother and then, over to me. "You will have to fiddle around with the wheel on the top to get them into focus", my brother yelled. At present, I was getting a blur of blue water. I got the hang of it with a bit of assistance and saw silver silhouettes reflecting the afternoon sun, slowly moving along the horizon. Battleships bristling with guns, towers and aerials; Cruisers and Destroyers, they looked ominous, one by one moving across the distant water. "Did you see the aircraft carriers Pete?" my brother taunted. "What's an aircraft carrier?" I yelled back. "The flat ones" he advised. I looked through the eye piece again, struggling with the focus. Yes, I did see a flat one, somewhat larger than some of the other ships, but no aircraft in view at that distance.

The vista became a formidable array of twenty to thirty warships, silver objects moving slowly across the horizon in a majestic procession.

The focus of attention continued for some time with binoculars being handed backwards and forwards, before a return to more holiday pursuits.

A day or two later it was time to depart, buckets and spades disappeared into the family holiday trunk which was customarily dispatched back via a carrier and would turn up a day or two after we returned home. Suitcases were also packed which came with us and the morning arrived when it was time to make our way to the railway station and onwards to London and then south to Sanderstead on the northern outskirts of Surrey. Travel was mainly by train. Motor cars were few and far between and the roof rack would have been a thing of the future. Air travel was practically unknown unless you were travelling overseas and even then, it I was reserved for the rich. We lived in the very early days of modern travel. We were a short taxi ride from the railway station at Gorleston. A tidy place with a close-cut privet hedge running full length at the back of the platform. The train was already waiting, gleaming green carriages fronted with an equally gleaming green and black steam locomotive, the logo for the London and North Eastern Railway (LNER).

Our father walked us along the platform to inspect the engine, a customary pursuit in those days, and if there was time on these occasions to be greeted by a cheery smile from the driver and his fireman. The engine hissed like a great cauldron and you felt the heat from the furnace. No wonder steam engines continue to be an icon even today with the modern generations. They did their job with formidable glory even if they showered us with dirt and pollution.

It was time to return to our seats to be greeted by an anxious mother craning her head out of the carriage window to see where we had got to. We settled down, whistles sounded along the platform, being blown with noisy enthusiasm by eager platform staff, whistles firmly gripped between their teeth, hands raised to signal the driver. We were on the move, slowly at first and then with comfortable speed the train pulled along the platform and out into the countryside, clouds or white smoke and steam rolled across the open fields as we headed south. We were on our way home.

War was declared on 3rd September 1939, but nothing much happened for many months, at least not on what was described as the 'Home Front'. Time moved on to Christmas and into 1940. The quiet period continued, apart from the occasional sporadic attacks by enemy aircraft particularly in the south of the country. There were frantic preparations taking place throughout the land to improve defences particularly airfields and military bases in anticipation of air raids on them. It was impossible to defend every vulnerable industrial area in the country from aerial bombardment, but much work was taking place to diversify production of military equipment and materials, particularly aircraft, the effort was huge and comprehensive.

I asked my father when was the war going to start, not that I really knew what to expect at that stage, I had no comprehension of it. I am sure he did not have much idea either, at least to the starting time; he was probably wondering himself. He had served in the infantry during the First World War, 25 or so years earlier and had fought and had been wounded at the Battle of the Somme in 1916.

War was no longer a stranger to him and as time went on he would illustrate how battle trained he was.

The Battle of Britain had yet to get underway and it was that summer it got started. There was a Sunday in August, a family walk had been arranged, it would not have been an ambitious affair, a stroll for a mile or two, perhaps to Sanderstead pond and back. A popular destination of the day for weekend walkers. My sister was in the push chair and we had turned into Victoria Avenue and were making our way to the Penworthan Road, the air was filled with the sound of an air raid warning siren. These melancholy instruments had been recently installed at locations spaced two or three miles apart throughout the district, in fact all over London. They became an unmistakable message of imminent aerial attack and probably bombardment, which was to reach considerable proportions in the months and years ahead. My parents broke into a run, with the rest of us, including push chair being dragged along with some urgency. It was realized that a new air raid shelter had recently been completed just beyond a road bridge spanning the Croydon to Tonbridge rail track on Purley Downs Road. As we crossed the bridge, which had taken several minutes of panic to reach, the sound of multiple aircraft engines could be heard coming from the south. We looked up to see a flight of Ju 87 Stuka dive bombers roar overhead, the full regalia of swastikas, black and white cross adorned the wings and fuselages of the planes. They had probably used the railway line to help navigate from the coast. They were flying low to escape newly located radar installations at the coast and along the way. I watched them bank to the left, cross the valley of South Corydon, and head towards Croydon Airport, just over the horizon, their gulled wings swaying as they receded from us. The planes were so low we could have easily been gunned down in the street but, no doubt, the pilot and their crew were too busy concentrating on their target to pay heed to us.

In the vicinity of the airport black objects fell from the underside of the planes, exploding in balls of red and black smoke, with accompanying explosions, there was no opposition.

There was sound of further planes approaching, my Mother dragged me towards the entrance of the shelter which was now filling up with frightened and anxious locals, coming in all directions, some from their homes, to the seeming security of the bunker. We sat facing one another on slatted wooden benches my nose filled with the cleansing smell of freshly laid cement and concrete, a reminder of its recent construction. We must have sat there for at least half an hour as the raid continued, until the more welcome sound of the 'all clear' siren was heard giving us leave to go. As we filed out my father insisted to continue the walk with my brother, but my mother had, not unnaturally, had enough and escorted the younger generation back to the house. The air raid shelter was demolished sometime after the war and this unused part of the golf course land was sold on for redevelopment into several homes which remain there today. It's possible that the owners there have little knowledge of the contributions that their front gardens made to the war effort and the sanctuary offered, no doubt, on numerous occasions. The airport was extensively damaged, as a result of this raid along with some adjoining factories, fifty or more were killed and even more injured, the following day a small group of us walked the two miles to the airport to see the damage. It wasn't a pretty sight and it was my first visit to a scene of war. Fortunately, the original terminal building was spared and remains there to this very day, now converted into a hotel, a fine example of 1920's commercial architecture, no doubt with listed status for its undoubted heritage value.

Croydon airport was a natural target for the Luftwaffe at this juncture, it had been London's main civil air transport terminal since civil airline operations began in the 1920's after the first world war so there must have been something prestigious in bombing it in these early days of conflict. Civil airline movements had ceased at this stage, but preparations were taking place for the airfield to be making its contribution to the air defence system. The Luftwaffe's aim was to destroy the Royal Air Force on the ground, which never happened but all airfields in the south of the country became legitimate targets for this. As the campaign continued and our air force gained in strength, week by week, in trained personnel, pilots of course and fighter aircraft to go with them; it became part of the art of survival to hide our planes in as many obscure corners of as many airfields as possible.

Croydon was not a primary base for much of the time and was never considered for bombers on account of its short grass runways and restrictive position. I recall Spitfires stationed there from about 1942 onwards. They would take off in volume, line abreast across the airfield and roar over the housetops on their interceptor missions, the main defences locally were provided by Kenley and the Biggin Hill airfields and both of these were in the front line of the aerial battles that swamped the skies in the coming weeks.

Croydon was a difficult airport at the best of times, it had a dip in the middle of the field itself and there were no hard runways although concrete spurs were built after the war was over to assist some of the heavier planes on a return to civilian operations in 1946 and it retained its status as London's main airport for a short while. It was surrounded by housing to the west and an industrial estate to the north extending for some distances and this is still in place today.

It was not long before airline operations were transferred to Heathrow which quickly became London's main airport, its magnificent runways used by heavy bombers during the war and needing the long runways to life their heavy, deadly loads for the raids on enemy targets. In those days, there were also two parallel diagonal runways in addition to the two east-west runways operational today to accommodate changes in wind direction affecting take offs and landings of the smaller and relatively lighter planes of the time. The diagonals were eventually taken out to provide space for the terminal buildings, hangers, taxi-ways and disposal areas that make up the modern airport in place today. Northolt airfield a few miles to the north of Heathrow, another RAF base during the war was also adopted for airline use during the formative post war era of airline operations, but returned to military status in the early 1960's.

Chapter 2

Battle of Britain

FOLLOWING THE RAID ON Croydon airport the Battle of Britain started in earnest. It was a battle, in the sky. It was a year of destiny for the country as the ensuing air attacks were a crucial part of Hitler's strategy to invade and conquer Europe and eventually achieve world domination. A lynchpin in the master plan was the elimination of Britain's infrastructure, along with the country's invasion and occupation and the preliminary ground work for this was the destruction of our struggling new war machine via heavy bombing of our industrial areas and the attempted demoralization of the civilian population; by heavy bombardment, particularly at night and the neutralize our air force along with our airfields.

Once this was over it should have been possible to send in an invasion force, ground troops and armour to take over the country completely, compromise the Empire, the largest in the world at that time, and remove from the reckoning a world power as he had managed to do with the occupation of France a year before. Therefore, the success or failure of this battle, this episode must determine the eventual outcome of the war. This was the thinking until it went drastically wrong for Hitler.

1940, to my recollection, was a mostly fine summer, blue skies in August and September, especially in our part of the world, where much action took place; Croydon and its environs, was not the whole scene but saw a great deal of action. The battle developed, and the visual spectacle in the sky unfolded. Schools were closed, daily attacks, many lasting for an hour or more, as enemy planes flew over to their targets, near and far across the south of the country before returning back to base.

Croydon and South London became the principal over fly zone and remained so throughout the war. Enemy war planes travelled from bases in occupied France, Belgium and Holland and further back from Germany itself. Their main strategic bomber force of the day comprised the twin engine Heinkel 111K, Dornier 215, both medium range and capacity bombers, escorted by the Messersmitt 109 and 110 fighters. The 110 twin engine was the faster of the two, the 109 being the most similar to the Spitfire, but smaller than the Hurricane, the Hurricane was the 'top gun', but a bit slower than its British companion and its German adversary, the 109. The Heinkels and Dorniers were relatively small aircraft and usually raided in scores if not hundreds in order to transport the volume of bomb they planned to drop.

Hurricane and Spitfire fighters were the chief defenders and challengers to the Luftwaffe's invading hordes and were the star players of the day. The Spitfires had the speed and manoeuvrability rising head and shoulders above the rival escorting Messersmitts, it was designed right for the time and was the cutting edge of technology in its day.

As kids we were out on the streets every day, full of excitement to witness some of the action, air raid warnings were usually followed by a delay before the bomber force made its way over to targets, mainly further inland; My friend, a few doors away, owned a blue bike, I recall, I had a red one, we only needed someone with a white one and we would have been flying the flag. On one such raid a flight of defending Spitfires took off from Kenley Airfield, the planes rising and turning east in dramatic urgency, first one and then another etc, their red and blue insignia clearly visible against the camouflage on the underside of their wings, the sound of their Merlins receding into the morning sky. We were having a busy morning and Kenley was at the forefront of the defensive action. After a short while we heard the sound of machine guns coming from the eastern sky and a plane veered into view trailing smoke. Some time later the defending forces returned to base, their day was no done until their success in the skies was acknowleged with a victory roll, qualifying pilots would climb, roll into an arc completing a circle before straightening up for touch down ; The performance entirely unofficial, of course, such elation no doubt helped to release tension from the conflict.

Each day there was a spectacle of engagement in the skies, the enemy Messersmitt fighters wheeling and dealing with Spitfires and Hurricanes, silver specs in the skies above, and to the east of us, not always shooting at each other over the urban areas, the fighter escorts waiting for the bombers return from targets inland. Much of the shooting would start over the open countryside of Kent, as the enemy formations were returning to base and were easy targets for our fighters, it had become a ballad of air combat before the killing started.

My Mother would appear at the garden gate, pale and ever anxious in these situations, 'I think it time you came in dear' my friend's Mother was giving him the same advice and as the morning continued ,the noise in the air grew louder and more intense. Under these circumstances 'going in' meant taking a place in the shelter, which in our house was taking a place in a cellar under the stairs, the safest place, not least in these early stages of the War; Like any cellar we would not have survived a direct hit, but it was protection from flying glass and debris from a nearby blast. We had had the cellar converted to accommodate three or four sleeping spaces as events eventually turned into night time raids, there was immediate access to the kitchen and out of the house if circumstances required it.

The battle in the air reached its climax on 18th August 1940, the heaviest and most turbulent enemy daylight raid so far. Croydon and the surrounding area were included in the battleground. The RAF fighters accounted for a record number of enemy planes that day, and marked a turning point in enemy bombardment... Hitler realized that our air defences had grown beyond his previous estimates and we have become a strong force. Our air force had not been wiped out, our airfields were far from being obliterated and the rising tide of newly completed Spitfires and Hurricanes, and other planes coming off the production lines had now become formidable opposition. The tapestry had come reworked and in addition to this, facilities of all kinds were improving on a daily basis, not least the supply of trained pilots and personnel. The tide of onslaught had been stemmed. The danger of imminent invasion by the German forces receded and then passed away.

Whilst the Battle of Britain was reaching its limits , the air war continued under the cover of darkness, but defences became less reliable and needed to be developed, in fact any targets on the ground were not easily identified after dark and there was a great deal of haphazard bombing with residential areas involved in attacks. Bombing also took place inadvertently over open countryside, on some occasions during daylight raids. It was not unknown for right minded raiders to unload bombs to get rid of them, if being pursued by our fighters after an unsuccessful raid. Our local golf course was heavily bombed on one occasion on account of this.

Air raids day and night, but predominately the latter continued for four years to the time of the invasion of France in June 1944. Raids continued after this time , but on a much reduced scale and included some innovative methods of bombing and attack which will be described later. Croydon and region remained one of the forefront areas for attack throughout this period f time , not least on account of a predominance of targets including airfields and light industry. London was always a primary target area even though it contained only a proportion of targets of legitimate interest and its easy first port of call location from enemy airfields in Europe.

A major attack on London (15th September 1940) inaugurated the 'Blitz'. This description characterised the continuous wartime bombing of London and became 'coined' for this episode of the war. The same date is now the commemoration day for the Battle of Britain.

German bombers of the day seemed to be powered by unsynchronised engines which emitted an eerie but distinguishable sound, it was important to know these things, after all, as a youngster, if you were walking home from school and got caught in an air raid you had to know who was about to fly over the tree tops. Enemy planes were not averse to gunning down the civilian population in the streets below and there were a number of instances of this happening around the area over the years. An acquaintance was attacked in a group, the veracity of the attack ripping up the roadway with bullets. The group survived the onslaught.

School would reopen for a spell and close again when things got bad, this situation prevailed throughout the war and we became used to 'no school' and lessons to be studied and worked on at home.

Air raid shelters were built in school grounds, at my particular school , there was a shelter in the school, by converting the main corridor, this was reinforced with substantial timber beams and supports, benches were provided to sit on. It offered an immediate central shelter quickly available from class rooms and was often needed in these precarious times.

Like all air raid shelters of the day, they would not be able to withstand a direct hit, from any bomb or missile, but they offered ample protection from flying glass and debris and machine gun attacks from the air. The underground subways and stations of the London Underground and Tube system was able to provide ample deep shelter protection from all kinds of conventional bombardment from the air and throughout the war, and particularly during the London Blitz, the local populations used Under round stations as their communal dormitory. against most close by eruptions and particularly flying glass, debris and falling buildings.

The sound of an air raid warning siren prompted an orderly evacuation from classroom to designated shelter under the guidance of tutorials. When everyone had settled down and the sound of gunfire and the drone of planes had entered the background, a large jar of sweets would appear, one each for a short raid but this 'ration' was doubled or trebled if the underground visit was prolonged The sweets accumulated from donations by parents over weeks and months from the meagre sweet ration that had been imposed by the government from early days

My mother started to make sweets at home to supplement the rationed supply, but it was a strain on the sugar ration, also in place, her contributions in this area were chocolate fudge and coconut ice presented on large baking trays and very much appreciated. I think these indulgencies were an improvement on anything that came out of the sweet coupons at this time.

Likewise, there were a few soft drinks available, to be bought in the shops, occasionally my mother would obtain a small supply of lemons and make jugs of freshly squeezed lemonade. Most fresh fruits from warmer climates were not available until after the war was over. The younger generation really did no know what a banana or a grape looked like. My father's advice stoic to the end, if you feel thirsty there's plenty of cold water in the tap.

Chapter 3

The Middle Years

EVERY MAJOR CITY AND conurbation in the country harbouring military and industrial targets were included in the Luftwaffe's hit list but the scale of enemy losses increased steadily and dramatically as the war continued. Some areas experienced relatively little bombardment and early in 1941 it was decided to evacuate, on the invitation of an aunt and uncle to the west midlands region of Kidderminster. We left the war zone for a period of safe sanctuary. My father stayed behind to look after the family home and maintain his job in London. He was called into ARP duties both at home and in London where he had to do an all-night fire watch, at least once a week, in one of the darkest areas of the city for destruction. The ARP (Air

Raid Precautions was a voluntary organization, locally consisted ten or twelve volunteers based in a convenient all night air raid shelter, usually located in the leading volunteer's back garden, and responsible for patrolling several local streets. The duties would be to attend dead and injured caught in a bombing, first priority, ensuring that all street lights were switched off, that every householder's blackout blinds were fully secured so not a trace of light escaped. This was always a very thorough operation throughout the war to ensure that enemy raids from the air could not possibly calculate where they were over Britain from the lights from towns and villages below. The night time tasks of these volunteers were considerable and they needed to patrol the district in strong coats and steel helmets to protect against falling shrapnel from our anti-aircraft gun batteries which were very active during air raids.

My aunt and uncle lived in Kidderminster a land of sugar beet farms and carpet factories, a far cry from the endless suburbs of South London. It was also a far cry from the air raid siren and the drone of enemy bombers not that we were completely devoid of the occasional attack, but they were few and far between. They owned a small house in a large garden, there was also a communal orchard beyond the garden, for young people it offered a remit to rural life that did not exist back home. My uncle taught me some gardening and how to grow vegetables. It was early spring time and the summer was coming, for a seven year old it was all a new experience. I was sent to the local primary school, uncle had a small Ford 8 which was running in spite of wartime austerities and dropped me off at the school 2 miles away every morning but it was my job to find my way back home in the afternoon. There were no buses on that route, the days were peaceful and the nights quiet. A considerable relief from the dramas and traumas of life around Surrey in the past year. Coincidentally my brother attended a local boarding school so we were able to see him at weekends. He had been dispatched to a safe place at the outset of war as parents decided what was going to happen and see the extent of events. We were to stay in Kidderminster for a whole year waiting to see how events were to turn out at home. As time went on raids on London levelled off and we returned. It was the end of 1941.

Evacuation life in Kidderminster had been a new experience at my time of life, new school and new friends, the attentions of a 'surrogate' father who had no children. He treated us like he would have done his own. I remember he made for me out of balsa wood, a model of an Avro Anson, a twin engine reconnaissance and light military transport aircraft of the day. It had been my birthday and I treasured it for many weeks before the wings dropped off trying to fly it. I suppose seven year olds do this sort of thing.

The decision to return to London was not taken lightly, the air war was still at high strength over the south east although the battle of Britain was over, as such, but it had not prevented the Luftwaffe from continuing night and day air raids although at a lower level most of the raids were night time and they were set to continue for several years. We did not know that at the time and we had not seen our father except for one short holiday to visit during the summer, against difficult and restrictive transport conditions. We had been refugees although fortunately our refugee status had no comparison to the bombed out homeless, penniless those who had lost loved ones in the carnage and destruction from enemy air raids.

Travelling back by train we had been able to see some of the devastation that had been taken place since we travelled this way before. What you were seeing from a railway carriage window as only a sample of what lay further afield. We entered the suburbs of London from the north west with unease as to what might lie in store in future weeks and months. At this stage in the war there was no let up and no anticipation of a turning point, if it was ever likely to exist. The short distance across London to Victoria station was achieved safely on the underground. The London Underground, a formidable ally was already telling its own tale and would be providing shelter and comfort to Londoners beyond the realms of transport. From Victoria, we took the train to Purley Oaks, our home environment, you couldn't call Purley Oaks a town or village as it was and is today, part of the urban sprawl that spreads for miles in every direction. We had a lengthy half hour stop in the middle of nowhere on this journey. An air raid was in progress this late afternoon and there was trouble on the line ahead. Eventually we reached Purley Oaks and arrived back to familiar surroundings. Two houses at the end of our road had been flattened and there was a crater in the road. A couple of hundred yards away to the south our house was still standing but some of the ceiling had reached the floor in the kitchen and kitchen windows had been broken and cracked. My father had filled the broken spaces with cardboard and covered the cracks with brown gummed strip.

There was not much chance of getting the glass replaced in the short term as there was a shortage of glass, putty and installers if you needed one. Brown gummed strip with the precursor of the modern day plastic based carton sealing tape, it was used extensively in those days to stabilise cracked windows and more particularly to criss cross window panes throughout the house to prevent breakage. Everywhere you went windows were taped up, not least to prevent flying glass that would afford nasty injuries in the event of a bomb exploding in the immediate vicinity.

My father as an executive in the paper industry, had access to supplies of paper and the gummed strip which his company manufactured. To the younger members of the family it afforded the occasional supply of writing and drawing paper which was otherwise in short supply. Newspapers were a mere shadow of today's productions amounting to perhaps four or six pages only for the daily read, advertising was virtually non-existent.

The fear of being bombed from the air was immediate and real, it was happening all around us. Croydon north and south was far from being the most devastated region although it was a primary route for overflying by enemy aircraft, up and down the country very many towns and cities were seeing extensive bombardment especially

London in the city and to the east where extensive raids became known as the blitz and the destruction became widespread. The expression of being 'bombed out' became coined for the reality of becoming homeless and a refugee with nowhere to go. It applied to factories and office. The situations was ongoing and people were being killed and injured on a considerable scale. If your place of work was destroyed and you survived the experience, you lost your job and faced a very uncertain future.

However, if the business and production lines could not be continued but you were in a position to carry on relocation to a safer part of the country became an option. It would therefore be necessary for employees to follow and this would probably be the male, head of the family, breadwinner, to secure livelihood and income.

Night time air raids continued to grow with steady intensity and the bombing attacks and blitz continued into 1942. Home in Sanderstead, my father had to consider the need for more adequate air raid shelter as there was no end in sight to the bombing raids. We graduated to a local public shelter for a while, a brick built structure with reinforced concrete roof and bunk beds to accommodate 30-40 local inhabitants. These shelters had been hastily built by local authorities over the past few months and were being located on any spare and bombed out land in the district. There must have been a steady building program as they began to appear in other parts. These shelters were not exactly a home from home but any form of luxury could not be expected. The lighting was poor, some occupants refused to go to sleep or even to bed for that matter and passed half the night engrossed in conversation. In the morning you had to get up early, roll up your bed and make your way home providing there was no air raid in progress. However, these shelters remained in being and continued to be used until the end of the war.

A number of different types of domestic shelters were being developed to protect an increasingly displaced and frightened population throughout the country. The Anderson shelter, presumably named after its creator, was a small family sized room approximately 12 feet x 10 feet, installed in the back garden, a hole in the ground covered with curved sheets of corrugated iron for primary protection and then covered with earth and landscaped with turf and a door at either end: it could not be seen from the air and became a complimentary part of the garden scene. It moved home dwellers from crumbling buildings and flying glass, in a bombardment there was also protection from shell casings, shrapnel from anti-aircraft shell busts from the guns below. Tons of small pieces of metal would rain down on to the ground from intensive anti-aircraft gun activity in the course of all night-time enemy raids. It meant that once you were in your shelter you had to stay there. Around the Croydon area there was a concentration of anti-aircraft guns and accompanying search lights throughout most of the war years. People spent much time in these shelters, day and night, they became furnished, decorated and made comfortable, part of the home.

Our coal cellar was finally deemed to be unsafe as a shelter and went back to storing coal. My father arranged to have a Morrison shelter installed and this arrived one morning in a kit form, which we put together ourselves. Morrison shelters were relatively small, but quite adequate, they were meant for indoor use only and had the advantage of indoor heating etc. during the winter months whereas outside shelters needed their own heating. The Morrison shelter was approximately 8feet x 6feet and constructed with four right angle corner posts, supporting a steel frame top and bottom, approximately ¼ inch steel sheet on top and wire mesh offering side protection all round. A wire mesh base provided support for mattresses etc. We slept there every night for the remainder of the war, and felt safer and more comfortable than the public shelters which continued to provide protection for many over the same duration.

Even the cat enjoyed the comfort of sleeping amongst three companions. My father continued to enjoy his own bed upstairs, in the danger zone, but then he was a seasoned warrior from the trenches during the first world war, and air raids none of them in Southern England night or day, posed for him the dangers he had encountered in the trenches of .1916.

For my mother and the younger members of the family our continuous wartime experiences provided ongoing danger. The air raid siren would usually send out its message around 9pm. It was not easy to sleep, and it was a case of lying in bed and waiting for the inevitable. A regular thought was – are we going to be killed tonight? Will I see my older brother again?

As an air raid progressed, on a clear night, powerful search lights located in different parts of the district would probe the sky for incoming enemy aircraft. The sound of them was loud enough, but actually locating the planes was not so easy. The search lights approximately 2-3 metres in diameter and a depth of a metre consisted of a reflector powering a beam of light through the lense and powered by a portable generator could be located anywhere. The light beam had very little spread and had the characteristic of a giant laser in the nature of its appearance (although of course laser technology had yet to be developed). A search light had its own platform and a turntable mounted on the back of a truck and the light beams would flash around the sky like waving a giant torch. They were a very impressive piece of equipment and an adversary caught in its relentless beam had no chance of escape and became hostage to the eager sights of the anti-aircraft gunner waiting below.

Anti-aircraft guns, like the searchlights were set up at strategic locations, not bunched together in the event of being targeted, mainly at local airfields but some were mounted on flat cars to run up and down the railway tracks firing on the move. On some occasions, you heard the sound of firing diminish as the unit was driven down the track. These operations were commissioned after the late trains had gone, there was no demand for late night train operations, most commuters had been glad to get home as early as possible and general travel was on a much reduced scale.

My mother decided to enroll at a small library located at a well-known newsagent. Public libraries were popular and in general use but inconvenient to visit without much local transport and the motor car was not in general use. We walked to the local shopping parade, she was able to borrow a book or two for a fee of a few pence per week. At the library check out I noticed a calendar showing each year up to 1945 and I asked her if the war would be over by 1945, she looked at me sadly and said she did not know, but we might be all under the control of the Nazis by then. Such was the tensions of war and living under constant attack from the air. Any hopeful speculation on this subject had to be qualified by the success of developing allied military operations. Europe was in the main, completely occupied by Nazi forces, they had moved their aerial strength to the extremities of their occupied territories with the additional strength of Mussolini's Italy. The sea lanes to Britain were now increasingly being hazarded by attacks from Nazi U boats on supplies of food and material, leading to a substantial volume of shipping being sunk as it approached our shores.

Kent and Surrey offered a broad access corridor to the country as a whole, no doubt the river Thames, 20 odd miles to the north acted as a navigation aid, a glistening ribbon of reflected light under a moon on a clear night. The bombers rolled on, the monotonous tone of their engines preceding the barrage of defense the rumbling noise of bombs hitting the ground, the whine of stricken aircraft and the raining of shrapnel from exploding gun shells. You did not want to be caught out in it.

The night raids continued on and off more or less continuously throughout 1942 and into 1943. They were of varying intensity and magnitude. I recall in 1943 a vast attack on Croydon with incendiary bombs, these were a relatively small device and the force of the blast was comparatively light but they spread fire, a small aircraft could carry scores, the larger bombers, hundreds. The raid lasted all night the continuous whistle of falling missiles, almost every home was hit, the following day, a Saturday, we toured the district to survey the damage, there were holes in the road and in the gardens and they fell through roofs of houses A friend's house received one through the roof and down the stairwell into the hall. It left a large hole in the hallway floor into the foundations. Fortunately, it didn't explode so the family were saved as there would have been no way out of the house through the front door. As we stared down the hole, bomb disposal arrived and yanked out the unexploded bomb and put it onto a waiting truck. Many were not so lucky and there were fires and reports of deaths and injuries everywhere.

From early 1942 school days returned in earnest. Aerial war had given over from daylight to darkness, it was not that there were no daylight attacks, but they were few and far between. it was possible to learn of the experiences of friends from more distant parts of the district. School in Sanderstead village was a bus ride away, about two and a half miles or a long walk. The walk was mainly in the afternoons in the summer, but not without marauding aircraft. Messersmitts darting in from occupied France on a hit and run. It was not the first occasion that I found myself crouching behind a garden wall on this journey during one such attack. The school situation remained fairly steady thought-out 1942 and into 1943. If an air raid occurred we would remove from the classroom to the shelter in the school grounds for half an hour or so, but there was no recollections of serious bombings in daylight and it remained just a disruption in the school day. As I moved up through the school it was alleged that my form mistress was a member of the secret service, she was a large robust woman who wore clothes not unlike a military uniform with squared padded shoulders. She was particularly stern and would disappear form weeks on end and then return to teaching. It was as reported that she had been on a mission and then returned to her civilian job for a while to wait her next assignment. She certainly looked the part and in these dark days there may very well have been much truth in this idea.

During the course of 1942 we began to experience a reversal of activities. Bomber command along with the US Air Force, our firm ally with its considerable and indispensable air power were about to enact the programme of reprisal on Germany. Together we had amalgamated the largest bombing force every known. Bomber command air fields had been developed or upgraded and suitable airfields had been located for the assignment of American war planes to lead the attacks. The homes for the heavies were in place and the daylight attacks were underway. The raids were on occupied Europe and particularly on the Nazi war machine of the Ruhr, where heavy industry was located and also on industrial zones thought the country. In the early stages these were relatively light assignments but there as a steady build up which continued into 1944. On account of the unique location of Surrey and South

London, we were in the transit zone to witness this dramatic new reversal of war in the air. Overflights from British and American bases, located in different parts of the South and South West England found their route across our skies, across Kent and on their outward journey to the targets of their assignments. Other routes embraced East Anglia attacking Germany from the north west.

The country was filled with encouragement and in the south east we were witnessing first-hand the 'turn of the tide' being proclaimed by our Churchillian government. After two and a half years of Nazi assault and widespread fear, there was now the inspiring roar of heavy bombers making majestic progress eastwards towards their targets. The highlight to these events was the 1000 bomber raid on Germany.

On one day the skies over Croydon and Purley were filled with planes on their outgoing mission as far as the eye could see, north and south and coming over from the west in groups of three or four planes, both the RAF and the USAF were in full strength. There were Lancasters, Stirlings and Halifax accompanied by the Liberators and Flying Fortresses of the USAF. The Flying Fortresses so named because of its comprehensive defensive system, incorporating machine gun turrets in the nose, tail, top and bottom of the fuselage and either side of the fuselage. Such a defensive system was necessary, when they reached the target zones they were to be encountered by the Messerschmitt's and the formidable FW 190 which had a comparable reputation to the Spitfire. I recall that one of our outgoing bombers, some miles to the south was trailing smoke that morning, obviously in a little bit of trouble and touched down somewhere to the east before it left our airspace. The outcome of the raid was well known and the Nazi war machine was coming under severe strain and was beginning to face an opposition it had not bargained for.

It was to be said that the air offensive from Germany to Britain was not over yet. Hitler had some more tricks up his sleeve and the south east of England would be targeted with new-fangled weapons and London and Surrey would be at the forefront of the target area. Conventional day and night bombing raids from the Luftwaffe would continue to diminish and school days would return to near normal for a while.

Chapter 4

The Night of the Doodlebug

1944 WAS TO HERALD a new phase in the war. An allied land invasion of France was on the cards, the long planned opening of the Western Front. There had been much planning for this event and many army units earmarked for this were stationed through the south east of England and Sanderstead and Croydon had its share of contingents. The air war over Britain was about to enter a new phase, much of it effecting London and the south east in particular and Croydon very much in the firing line.

The D-Day landing somewhere in occupied Europe had been anticipated for some time, no one, of course, as to where and when this would take place. Russia had been pressing for some considerable time that this event should take place, to relieve the armies in the east. The Russians were making substantial progress with their armies, advancing across the country with some of the biggest land battles in history, the biggest tank battle took place that year resulting in a Nazi retreat, and large numbers of prisoners were taken. The tide had turned in 1942, at the Battle of Stalingrad, when Russian forces finally stemmed the Nazi advance. Russian was taken aback by the initial invasion but had considerable resources in manpower, and its vast territories. It is difficult to imagine how Hitler ever thought he could conquer a country stretching over ten time zones even if he had the troops Russia had, from Russia's180 million population.

Russia, with great speed, and much help from the western allies moved its industries and war machine to the east beyond the Ural Mountains and well out of the reach of Luftwaffe bombers. Russia also had assistance with supplies of aircraft, tanks and military equipment of all kinds, which clearly helped its capabilities. Much of the equipment was shipped via the Arctic convoys from Britain and up the Norwegian coast to the Arctic sea and on to the seaports of Murmansk and Archangel. It was a considerable sacrifice on our part as many vessels and supplies were lost to German U boats in these northern waters. An elderly friend of mine testified to the hardships as he was on several cargo journeys through the area, but ultimately returned with his life intact. Crews of these Arctic convoy cargo boats were unsung heroes of the day.

The western allies had been biding their time to select the best time for the invasion. Up until then our main land effort had been from North Africa through Italy, but clearly our land battles had not been on the same scale as those experience by Russia in the east.

The 6 June 1944 was a fine summer morning as I recall, a brief announcement on the early morning BBC news offered the terse announcement that allied forces had landed in Normandy east of Cherbourg. There wasn't a lot of other information to hand other than that the invasion was going according to plan. The invasion was an enormous event by any standards, it had been anticipated for at least two years and there had always been speculation as to when and where it would be. After the usual morning assembly, we made it to the class rooms whereupon our teacher insisted that we stand for a brief prayer for the success of the long awaited invasion and for the good fortune and progress of the Allied forces. This even was the lynchpin to the beginning of the end of the war. Britain and Allies had to free enemy land forces from occupied territory which was practically the whole of Europe apart from Sweden, Switzerland and the Iberian Peninsula. Allied forces had been advancing through Italy for some time but this was small potatoes compared to the much larger campaign needed to clear Nazi forces from the whole of France, the low countries, most of Scandinavia and occupy Germany itself. Russian forces were advancing rapidly from the east, but it was no plan to let them do the job for us.

The invasion itself was across the English Channel from the south coast, invasion troops were crammed into landing craft and on the morning had to travel the eighty to ninety sea miles, to establish a land bridge head on the coast to the west of the city of Caen they were fully supported by allied naval and air forces. Much of the invasion force set from as far west as Dorset, the buildup had been spread along the south coast for security and practical reasons, it had not been anticipated that everyone should arrive in France at once and there had been considerable efforts to avoid high concentrations for forces in one area, not least to keep the enemy guessing and to avoid an enemy blitz on any concentration of military personnel and hardware.

Sanderstead, South Croydon and Purley had been host to army forces for about two years, houses had been requisitioned for military use all over the area and I remember detachments of troops assembling at the end of streets each day and marching in the middle of the road to the communal canteen, a church hall adjacent to St Mary church in Purley Oaks Road. Purley Beeches in Beech Avenue was closed and had been requisition by the military to park up Bren gun carriers, a small open tracked vehicle and supply lorries in sizeable numbers. These were regularly camouflaged under the huge beech trees from enemy air reconnaissance and a mixture of aggregate and cinders was laid down on the broad pathway through the woodland to avoid vehicles bogging down in the mud. The temporary road was never cleared up in the years after the war and might still be lying around today, or some evidence of it. All these activities attracted the full attention of the younger members of the local population and good relations were established between the locals and the visitors, we were all in it together, in one form or another and looking forward to the end of the war. It must have been at some stage during the month of May, all the military suddenly disappeared and there was a vacuum although nothing was understood of this exit but no doubt they had moved to the south coast to join the invasion forces. There must have been similar exits from districts all over Surrey and beyond as the invasion armada was assembled.

Prior to D-Day and form some weeks it was customary for the BBC to issue messages to underground forces, allied to allied western armies to undertake pre-arranged operations of sabotage against the Nazi occupying troops, particularly in France were the anticipated invasion was to take place. My recollection is that these instructions were issued over a period of 15 to 20 minutes prior to the 6 o'clock news, although they might well have been broadcast at other times. The format of these coded messages would normally be a short but entirely illogical phrase such a 'a happy penny that strikes the key board' or 'the black cat burrowed under the oak tree' etc., all completely different and making no normal sense, they would be in English and an instruction to the recipient group of saboteurs to immediately carry out a pre-arranged task, this might be to blow up a bridge over a particular stretch of road, that might normally be used as a key route, used by enemy occupying forces to transfer supplies to a potential front line position etc. the amount of pre-arranged action of this kind prior to actual invasion must have been considerable and would have provided a substantial contribution to the success of the invasion and establishing the necessary bridgeheads for the allied forces to move on.

These 'fifth column' organization would have become well established since the time of the original Nazi occupation and may very well have been operated on a part time basis, in many areas, but their purpose was to build up a reservoir of information on the activities and movements of troops and equipment and liaise with allies in the UK particularly in planning any military operation.

The D-Day landings and the invasion of France had taken over as the leading subject of excitement and interest amongst the public population on the home front; Luftwaffe attacks from the air continued these were mainly at night time, as the daylight sky over the country was under the control of our air force. Following D Day the month was to reveal a counter attack to the invasion to be visited upon the home front. The Nazi war machine had new modern weapon systems and the time had arrived for them to inaugurate the new technology and test its effectiveness on the diehard British across the channel.

As with many nights in the previous two years or so I was in the habit of waking to the sound of a warning siren and the inevitable sound of incoming enemy planes and the sound of anti-aircraft guns and explosions. On this occasion the warning came later than usual it was followed by squadrons of incoming planes that seemed to be flying to targets beyond us with their regular engine sound. There was also a new sound coming from the sky it was like a two stroke motorcycle engine passing overhead and at a much lower altitude than the regular aircraft, in fact the sound was just overhead. There seemed to be quite a regular flow of these unfamiliar visitors and then, occasionally the engine would cut out, followed shortly afterwards by the rumbling explosion associated with the bomb or plane crash.

After a while I knew something was radically wrong or radically different. We were under attack from the world's first cruise missile. This was the inauguration and we were the unwilling recipients. Croydon was clearly one of the initial target areas and just within range of the launch sites, although most of London was about to be engulfed with the onslaught which was to continue for some weeks, night and day. It had the characteristics of a continuous air raid. It needed only one missile casually launched racing across Kent at over 400 mph to cause an air raid warning along the route and everyone to take cover. The launch sites were in Calais and surrounding area.

The missile was a 30' long tube enclosing 1000lbs of high explosive, streamlined nose-cone balanced for flight by two short span wings mid-way along the length and a powerful enough ram jet mounted on a pod on the tail end. It was launched from ramps by catapult with sufficient force to provide speed to fire up the ram jet promptly and take it at over 400 mph across the English Channel into Kent and Surrey, and when the fuel tank was empty it just dived into the ground and if you were in the way you had had it. There were no guidance systems as we know today, nothing had been invented. Guidance was the direction of launch and range was determined by the amount of fuel in the tank. If it had had more time for development it would clearly have become a deadlier weapon with accurate targeting. Subsequently its life was short lived as the allied advance through to Northern France post D-Day eliminated the launch sites. It was not a vehicle for a much longer range without compromising its bomb load and speed. The existing rage was 100-150 miles which brought it within the range of the heavily populated areas and it was therefore a terror weapon and an indiscriminate killer.

By 6am that day, they were still coming over, there must have been dozens, even hundreds that night and into the morning, there was a respite for an hour or two around breakfast and then the onslaught continued.

A solemn radio announcement at news time informed us that we were under attack from a new type of weapon, when an air raid siren forewarned of an attack we were advised to take cover or get in a shelter because the bombing was indiscriminate and deadly. The machines was described as a 'flying bomb', later named a 'buzz bomb'. The official title later announced as the V1. Nazi broadcasts gleefully announced possession and use of this weapon that would turn the tide of the war. The designated V1 implied that there may be more variants or variety of weapons to come. V for Vorsicht translated as 'look out' – 'danger' would have been an appropriate prefix to designate their new weapon. There is no doubt that the Germans had made huge advances through science in weapons and methods of propulsion for aircraft in particular; so indeed, had the Allies. Britain and American in particular, it required the frantic urgency of multiple conflict in warfare and the prospect of imminent invasion, to draw on all the resources of inventiveness and ingenuity to advance the hardware of warfare. The German nation was slightly ahead of us in the development of the jet engine for planes and other methods of propulsion, fortunately the Nazis were somewhat more behind in the development of atomic weapons, we would have otherwise needed to face a secret weapon of catastrophic proportions.

On the first morning of the attack apparently a reporter had the opportunity to see one of the new missiles during an air raid whilst on his way to work. He grabbed a scrap of paper and "doodled" an image of the craft as it went by, doodling" was a buzz word of the day, to make a sketch of an object. There were no instant cameras in those days, in the normal course of events, so his inspired action was an adequate substitute as the opportunity had been presented .Later he showed his "doodle" to colleagues who presumably had not yet had the opportunity to see one for themselves and they remarked that it looked like a bug. Hence the slang title "doodle bug" was commissioned as a title for the new flying bomb hitting out shores. In news items which followed this somewhat informal colloquialism describing the V1 took hold and the title became generally accepted even to this day.

This new event was about to transform life for some while as the days progressed, Doodlebug attacks were on-going, limited by Nazi production hold ups as the numbers being fired at us had been considerable. Due to the haphazard nature of the attacks, once again, schools had to close but every effort was made for schoolwork to be set for school children to work at home and there was some uncertainty, reinforced later, as to when school would restart. Classroom attendance was a hazardous prospect under the threat of intermittent air strikes which might only last for a few minutes, whereupon everyone needed to take cover, air raid shelter essential only to be visited by another raid half hour later. The following week we were all called in for a short while to be given work that could be completed at home, we were given an additional quota the following week and this went on for some time. The V1 raids continued for some weeks night and day. School attendance continued to be sporadic and the family speculated on another evacuation.

A major problem for air defence was how to intercept and stop the Doodlebug. With a ground speed in excess of 400mph it became a task to chase and shoot them down even in broad daylight and it needed to be in open countryside. The anti-aircraft gun was pretty limited and could only take pot shots at them at these speeds. The Spitfire was operating at the limit of its top speed even to keep up with them quite apart from take aim and fire.

The Spitfire could only attack successfully in a shallow dive to provide adequate speed, stability and steady aim, this had its drawbacks and risked firing towards the ground with consequences for those people and their property on the ground below. Better interception was achievable when the new Hawker Tempest fighters were brought in with a top speed of 500 mph but the 'piece de resistance' was the intervention the new Meteor jet fighter with its top speed of over 600mph, the record Doodlebug kills rose rapidly with the possibility to explode the entire machine in flight and minimizing the fallout of damage on the ground below. The ideal in this exercise, was interception over the Channel, soon after launch, with the whole lot exploding over the water.

The jet engine had been progressively developed in secret from the early days of the War from the invention by Frank Whittle and the Meteor was designed and built around the developed prototype engines by the Gloster Aircraft Co. the Meteor was given two engines although really only a fighter plane, and in 1946 broke the world air speed record, achieving a speed of 606 mph over the Thames estuary. A week later this was increased to 616 mph over the same course. The record did not survive indefinitely as the race was on both sides of the Atlantic to produce bigger and faster jets, culminating in the technology used on civilian aircraft for airline use in the 50's and 60's.

The Luftwaffe was operating its own jet fighter during the latter stages of the ward and even a rocket propelled fighter which operated against Allied bombers during the innumerable dog fights as Allied aerial armadas plundered Nazi targets.

In a sense, the Doodlebug campaign was a new Battle of Britain, in the latter stages of the war it did not have the same scale as the intensive daylight raids of the Luftwaffe in 1940, but as a terror weapon it had a dimension of its own.

As the military buildup in France continue and the military bridgehead became established and extended, so the air attacks over London and the south east intensified, an increasing number of V1's were appearing, they had the advantage to be unaccompanied thus releasing

Luftwaffe pilots for other activities, not that the Luftwaffe was enjoying great success as the skies were now in the hands of Allied planes. Rocket firing Typhoon and Tempest fighter aircraft, considerably faster and more powerful than the Spitfires and Hurricanes were ripping up Nazi ground forces in France and Belgium and along with their older counterparts dominated the skies. The Meteor jet fighter and its newly arrived accomplice the DE Havilland Vampire were rampaging their own targets and were very effective against the Doodlebug. However, the Doodlebug was making hay while the sun shone and raids were becoming more frequent and dangerous, they flew low and reached the ground with their package of destruction, at great speed once their fuel ran out. I think Sanderstead must have been more or less at the end of their range and along with Croydon received a lot of hits. I remember, with my father on the family allotment, one ceased its engine power overhead and made a steep decline in our direction, it was necessary for me to make a dive over a fence and slide down a railway embankment to comparative safety; although my father was not in so much of a hurry, being battle hardened in the trenches in 1916, he had seen plenty of danger and was used to it, he had been a great example and comfort on many occasions with a 'sang froid' attitude to danger. He was able to offer shouts of encouragement as I made my way to my idea of safety.

In the latter part of June, a second family evacuation was put into operation, again excluding my father and brother. My mother's brother in West Wales agreed to us staying with them for a while whilst the war moved on in every direction in the South East. My Uncle owned a farm on a small peninsula on the western end of Pembrokeshire, with eight cousins in the one family whom my sister and I had never met, I don't believe our mother had met them either as she had not seen her brother for 20 years, it was going to be a new experience for all of us, and they were to learn first-hand about a war that had hardly touched them

The arrangements for this second evacuation were finally settled, our mother, sister and myself accompanied by father, at least as an escort, as far as Paddington station in west London. Whereupon we were left to our own devices, en route to Pembroke. By all accounts it was a typical refugee operation although our mother had bought a hat for the occasion, no doubt to impress her long lost brother, unfortunately the hat became lost on the journey, which to some extent was understandable, as refugee trains go, this one was overcrowded in the extreme, short of people travelling on the roof as in some parts of the world and it left Paddington 4 hours late.

Paddington station itself was packed, there were trains leaving at intervals to all parts of the country served from it. There was not a bit of spare space anywhere on the platforms or the concourse leading to them, we joined a crowd or the queue leading to our assigned platform, there was no train to be seen and this was to remain the case for some time. There was no food either but some packets of sandwiches diligently prepared by our ever caring mother. We were informed our train had been cancelled for the original 11am departure and it was now rescheduled for

3pm on another platform, which for the time being was unapproachable for crowds waiting for earlier departures. Sometime later there as an air raid siren, forewarning of a new drama, a minute or two later we heard the now familiar sound of a Doodlebug making its way in our direction. The noise getting louder every second, suddenly the engine stopped and everyone in the station knew anything could happen. As far as the eye could see, and all around us 5000 travellers simultaneously crouched, at the prospect of being immediately bombed, but trained and disciplined response to commands, on horse guards parade, on a festival day, would not have emulated the discipline of that mass crouch by so many people at one time. A few seconds later there as a formidable rumbling explosion, so some poor devils got it, but for us a reprieve. Unfortunately, we had several more hours to wait in this vast and vulnerable cavern, before we could move on.

Eventually our train left the station and made its way, slowly, through the suburbs of north west London, bombed and damaged buildings were everywhere, we then reached open country and eventually Reading. It was a stop-start journey beyond to next stop Swindon, we all sat in the corridor on suitcases for that part of the journey but people got out and there was a seat for my hard pressed mother and then for the rest of us.

After Swindon it became more like a regular train journey, sandwiches were being consumed in greater comfort and proper seats to sit on, characterizing what the long distance traveler would deem to expect. We approached the Severn railway tunnel, an elderly fellow traveler leaned over and offered me the news that the tunnel was the longest rail tunnel in Britain and several miles long. I think I was filled with childhood awe at this as the train rumbled through the endless darkness.

We then came to Wales as my confidante had promised and then we were in Cardiff, after Cardiff we seemed to stop at every station, adding and subtracting passengers as we went, eventually a setting sun began to play on the pink granite embankment of the railway cuttings which seemed to go on for a long time, offering a display of colours giving an eventful day, contrast, and some peace from the fears of air raids and falling bombs. My mother was surprised I had noticed the colours, but they were calming the day for everyone in the compartment and I was contemplating the prospect of what was to come. Eventually the train was going to Milford haven which I had never heard of, but our destination of Pembroke was before that, enquiries revealed that we needed to change at Whitland, another obscure destination to my Croydon mind, and then, presumably, catch a train to Pembroke or Pembroke dock. As it turned out, we weren't told any of this at Paddington, but in the chaos of London under siege of constant war from the air, it's surprising that trains ran at all. We caught the Pembroke train from Whitland after a longish wait and trundle d along to the end. My Mother had no idea about the area but we found a taxi to take us the final three miles to my Uncles. Darkness had set in; the day was done and it was pitch black.

My Uncle and family lived in a remote farm house, and farmed the surrounding fields, beyond the village of

Hundleton towards Freshwater Bay and the seaside village of Angle. Our arrival, late that evening gave rise to much speculation and we were shown into the living room, a kindly aunt gave us a huge smile and our cousins, all six of them, filled with awe and curiosity at the new arrivals, sat on bench seats long the walls of the room, a door at the end lead into the kitchen and beyond whilst a substantial grate, with fire at full strength, divided two black painted oven on either side. A kettle whistled from a perch on the blazing fire and eventually my mother had a cup of tea, richly deserved after such an awesome journey.

We eventually learned that the fire in the grate had remained lit for several months, and while it was a warm summer evening in June the fire was the source of all cooking in the farmstead and fed all eight occupants night and day. The main source of fuel was wood and that was in plentiful supply. The main source of light, after dark were paraffin lamps and they accompanied us wherever we went. Life was basic and had not altered for many generations. The water supply came from a well outside the backdoor, all water for washing, cooking and drinking had to be drawn from the well in buckets and the toilet facilities was a privy beyond the extensive vegetable plots at the top of the garden, so getting out in the middle of a stormy night was an experience.

Baths were in a metal tub on the sitting room floor, all the hot water for this even needed boiling on the range fire so baths for eleven occupants of the house needed careful planning. In a short space of time we visitors from afar, driven by war, had moved from the suburban luxury of

Croydon to a third world we were to get to know in the coming weeks.

Three of my cousins, Sheila, Evelyn and Belinda were in charge of the catering which included cooking all the meals on the range, they were young teenagers but their skills in these task were considerable, they had been taught from an early age all they needed to know. The eldest of them, Sheila produced the finest fruit tarts you ever tasted, tops of pastry beautifully glazed with butter, fruit from the garden, and the hedgerows in the fields, cooked to perfection in an oven fired with wood. All the baking and roasting came the same way and their knowhow tempered with experience and practice from an early age. All food was sourced from the farm, the milk from the cows was to drink and make butter which was churned in the dairy, a room next to the kitchen. I remember several times, when chicken was on the menu for Sunday lunch, a young male cousin would go into the yard and grab a couple of chickens for the roast, do the necessary, pluck them with spirited banter and hand them over to the chef of the day for roasting. On many occasions it was deemed to be my task to peel the potatoes which for eleven people was a bucketful for roasting and boiling. It was a healthy life and apart from items like sugar and flour, the world of food rationing was treated with wry humour.

The following morning we got up to inspect our new surroundings, in a matter of 24 hours we had moved from war to peace, the war zone we had left behind was replaced by a region that had never known the war. My two eldest cousins had been called up to serve in the military and were stationed abroad. I believe there had been an air raid on Pembroke dock at an early stage of the war, but the area was too far for enemy bombers and there were few, if any strategic targets to be found on this remote peninsula. There was one possible exception. Milford Haven Sound was given over as a base for Sunderland flying boats, helping to secure the Atlantic approaches against enemy ships and submarines. The Sunderlands were used for air reconnaissance over the Bristol Channel, Irish sea and in to the eastern Atlantic and were constantly on patrol. We would watch them from the farm on their regular journeys, taking off and landing on the calm waters of the Sound. Our environment had been transformed to a near silent countryside, hearing only the sounds of the farm, the slow movement of cattle brought in for milking, the squabbling of chickens and pigs in the yard and dogs barking near and far. There was very little motorized traffic, a bus ran to and fro once a week, on market day, in Pembroke and if you missed it you had to walk or wait for the postal van that carried about five passengers in the back and ran a couple of hours later. My aunt and uncle's personal transport of the day was a horse drawn trap, this was brought out on rare occasion for family trips around the coast and the occasional visit into town. So we were isolated but we had our two feet, The village school was almost a mile away and I was enrolled there at an early stage, although it was only a few weeks before the summer holidays intervened. The summer holidays arrived late in the area, possibly to enable young people also to help on the farms over the harvest period. Journeys to school were a walk along a country road with cousins. The school was so small we had just one huge class, with the headmaster conducting all our activities. It was a far cry from my school in Sanderstead but it was free from the threat of air raids and the air raid shelter was not needed.

Life in this quiet farming community had not altered for many generations, my uncle had been born and brought up here although mother and the rest of her brothers and sisters were from Bath, the family home. After the end of WWI my uncle returned to the area and rented some land, to start a farm. Eventually he was able to buy additional land and expand his farming domain, but the early days were hard and much of the land needed development from scratch, it was customary during these hard times to have large families, not least to help with the labour force and doing work that was largely manual, it needed years of effort to bring such underused land to full production, and carve out markets for the produce. Eventually they were able to buy a farmhouse and expand their holdings.

Farming between the wars, and as we found it, was governed by the seasons and required no other authority, except harvesting crops at the end of the season and the farmer and his team were motivated to this target. The quality and preparation of the land for the growing season was paramount and occupied the autumn and winter months, also the selection of suitable fields for what needed to be grown and setting aside fields best suited for grazing. Farming was spread across the range to embrace dairy products, grain and vegetables, pigs for the slaughter and eggs for the market. This was to ensure a spread of income across the seasons and diverse the wits and activities of all involved. It was an endless task and the day began early and ended late.

As the summer approached Autumn, the harvesting got under way and there were several fields of grain that had to be cropped, in those days a combined harvester was hired for the essential task, starting along the edge of the field and then working its way round in a circle until it reached the centre where all the rabbits had congregated in fear of the approaching machines, but unfortunately there was really no escape. It then became the task of my cousins, not that much older than me, in years, armed with the family shot guns to slaughter all the rabbits they could for the dinner table. We could never go hungry and rabbit pie was the order of the day for some while. Potato and cabbage fields needed weeding and later harvesting, all by hand and my child labour was involved also to help with a task that became as endless as the day was long. It was a sharp contrast to life back home in Croydon.

At lunch times my cousins Evelyn and Belinda would appear carrying a tea urn between them and Sheila would walk behind them carrying a hamper filled with homemade bread sandwiches filled with thick rashers of farm prepared boiled bacon, a regular diet of the day. A table cloth laid on the stubble, a time honoured feature of a country life picnic in olden days. This went on over several days as harvesting continued and the barn was full. The war zone was a long way off. It was hard work but we were enjoying ourselves.

At the beginning of September we had to return to the village school for the autumn term, my uncle needed to hire labour to continue the harvest: later that month the air war over southern England eased brought about by the continued allied advance across Europe

The V1 bases were being overrun, at least around the primary north West France launch sites, and the threat had turned a corner. There was an imperative for us to return home to Surrey, not lest for my sister and I to continue our schooling and what might follow in this area. Enough school dates had been lost or compromised in recent years, the war was beginning to ease towards victory, although it wasn't over and there were more challenges to come. In the middle of September our farming adventure came to an end and we reluctantly had to depart from the new found family, just over three months of life changing experiences of how life in the heart of the country had compared to modern urban life close by one of the largest cities in the world. We boarded the train at Pembroke, backed by a family send off, the brown and yellow coaches of the Great Western Railway and headed back to Paddington. This time it was a departure far less onerous and delayed to the one we had experienced in the early summer.

We returned to Sanderstead, several houses had been destroyed at the top of the road on account of a Doodlebug whilst we were away and several other roads had been hit around the district, the cat was still at home, obviously a great survivor and our village primary school was still intact. We returned to school full time and were able to swap adventures with old school friends with many evacuation stories. The security situation had improved and it was possible to have uninterrupted days in the class room. There continued to be night time bombing raids and the Luftwaffe had taken to launching the Doodlebug from the top the Heinkel bombers, flying in across the Thames Estuary from Holland so the threat from the air was not over but was not so intense: the heavily laden Heinkel was a slow and lumbering craft readily vulnerable form the waiting Spitfires. It was for this reason that attacks were rescheduled after dark and were entirely random and indiscriminate, it was on one such night in September that a local orphanage was hit with the loss of many young lives, no military target there. From the Nazi point of view the advantage of launching the V1 Doodlebug in this way was that the ram jet already had the advantage of speed of over 200 mph on top of the bomber, so that it could fire up for a quick get away. Much of the bombing was directed towards London from the Thames estuary whereupon the Heinkels could turn round and make a speedy get away, These attacks were relatively short lived and were about to be superceded by another of Hitler's secret weapons

September was giving way to autumn and the month was reaching its end, it was a Sunday morning and we were about to be besieged by a new drama. My father and sister had taken a bus ride to Thornton Heath to visit friends. My mother and I stayed behind,, she upstairs and me downstairs. The air was filled with a faint whistle which grew steadily louder and nearer, the end game was a huge explosion, shaking the house and breaking a number of windows. My mother leapt down the stairs and grabbed me, pushing us both behind the substantial settee which was then doubling as an air raid shelter. I think she was expecting another explosion , as in the regular reception of a stick of bombs, but this was not to happen., we had been attacked by the world's first ballistic missile the V2. The news came through, quite soon, that a V2 rocket had targeted us about a quarter of a mile away on the edge of Purley Beeches with Purley Oaks Road, two houses had been entirely destroyed as they had received an almost direct hit, unfortunately two elderly occupants had been killed. Surrounding houses had been damaged, not extensively as the main force of the blast went into the woods, huge beech trees with girths of many feet were reduced to matchwood and several acres of woodland were flattened. A few months earlier the army would have been in occupation storing their vehicles but these 'birds had flown'.

Further down the road St Mary's Church was damaged at the south end and needed heavy wooden props to support the wall until repairs could be undertaken several years later. The back of the scout hut,facing the blast had caved in and required several weeks of diligent effort, on the part of the scouts to restore, no outside contractors available in those days. After the war, war damage repairs for everyone, became a long process unless you could do it yourself. This air raid was another pointless, random, attack, but there were many more to follow.

The V2's were launched from the relative safety of Holland and Germany and it would be some time before allied armies would reach their launch sites, but Allied air bombardments intensified and helped curtailment. The V2 had a 1 ton warhead and reached 50 miles altitude before descending to target at several thousand mph There was no defence against it, no anti-missile missiles in those days .it was unlikely you would ever see it but you might get an ever noisier whistle before it reached you.

The V2 was a liquid fueled ballistic missile with a conventional high explosive warhead in terms of modern day ballistic weapons it was rudimentary with next to no guidance system. It relied on pointing in the right direction and laden with sufficient fuel to provide range needed which wasn't more than a few hundred miles from the north European launch sites. Hitler had developed this weapon in the intervening years of the war and managed to get it going during 1944 just as the war was coming to an end. Attacks on Britain started in earnest in the September and continued regularly for a few months until the launch sites were destroyed by allied bombing raids or allied ground forces caught up with them as they advanced north.

Schooldays returned in earnest but life in the classroom was punctuated with long rumbling explosions, sometimes occurring several times a day as the Nazis continued to launch as many missiles as they could in random attacks across London and the south East of England. There was not a lot you could do about it, there were no air raid warnings, no air raid shelters that you could get to in time, if you were hit you were finished. It was an unnerving experience.

In the early part of 1945 the attacks ceased, life was beginning to take on a new phase and becoming more relaxed, the streets were no longer covered with shrapnel, day and night time bombing raids by enemy aircraft had now all but ceased although there was one incursion. Walking home from school, late afternoon when I had to take cover behind a garden wall as an enemy fighter came over on a strafing raid before being chased off. These were last desperate efforts on the part of the Luftwaffe as the Nazi forces were being pushed back by allied armies, there was a counter attack, the battle of the bulge, when the German army launched an attack of considerable proportions as we were about to enter Germany and it took some weeks before it was repulsed fully and the advance continued.

A young neighbour, Gordon living further along the road had been drafted into the military the previous year, he came home on leave in full regalia, with army kit, we met him on the road one morning, a crowd of eager youngsters plying for first hand news of battle. He told us he was on embarkation leave for a special mission, we crowded round pressing him for more information, which was clearly not forthcoming, he had a large commando knife stuck in his belt and we stood in awe until he had to part company with us indoors. We never saw him again, he was killed at Arnhem in September 1944.

As the Allies advanced into Holland and east across the Rhine into Germany itself, autumn became winter and winter into spring. The enemy sky had become less threatening and gave way to friendlier skies, they were being patrolled by the new generation of aircraft; the fighter jets.

Meteor and Vampire fighters whistled overhead proudly showing who was now in charge, they made quite a spectacle in their silver livery, and the whistle of their engines. They moved much faster than their traditional counterparts, flew at higher altitudes and left a vapour trail across the sky. This was new technology, the cutting edge had moved forward it was the debut of a new world.in the air.

During my spare time I spent many hours with my father on his allotments, he was an avid gardener and from early in the war he had taken up the mantle of 'dig for victory' to produce as much homegrown food as possible. During the early part of the war this was much encouraged as no one was certain if we were going to get enough to eat, during the process he produced ample fruit and vegetables, particularly the latter, fruit came later when he developed the larger of his two allotments into a miniature orchard.

One of my regular tasks in exchange for a weekly supply of pocket money, was assisting on the allotments digging and cutting the grass around the perimeter. The Nazis were soon to be defeated and we were all contemplating the end of the war and a new future opening up. I was thinking about future education, my primary school days were coming to an end and exam times were on the horizon, a milestone I had not had to think about before, but it had become the talking point amongst family and friends.

It was late spring 1945,and late one afternoon I was up to my old task on the allotment having walked down on my way home from school and no homework, or tea in sight for an hour or so, I did my chore and lay on the cut grass for a rest. The sound of a plane reached my ears, it was a heavy aircraft, so defined on account of its four engines and the deeper sound that they created, defining in those days the kind of aircraft involved and even its make and description, very often long before you saw it. It was approaching from the east, some distance away the sound from its engines getting closer, it was obviously at great altitude and travelling at slow speed. 250mph was a good speed for heavies, in those days but their sound was heavy.

The vapour trail came in sight at last, I could see it, a silver shape, making its way across the sky towards the west. The sky was clear and sun beginning to set. I watched it until it was out of sight making for wherever it was going; I continued to hear its sound for several minutes and strained my ears but I could hear it no more. It was like the last plane returning from the War and in no hurry to reach its base. The war was over. I savoured the quietness of the afternoon. Soon there would be celebrations all over Britain, and all over Europe, The war would continue against Japan, in the Far East, for some time. Their war machine was deemed to be finished and exhausted. Although they continued with the Battle, albeit on their own and the end game was uncertain

The long years of the War in Europe were behind us. It was 1945, the calendar in the bookshop had yielded its destiny. I got up from the ground and returned the tools to the shed, walked to the end of the field and out into the road. I was on my way home and to a new future.

Afterthoughts

The war in Europe came to an end in June 1945 and Nazi Germany had to surrender to Allied forces. Soldiers of the Western Allies (Britain, United States and France) shook hands with their counterparts in the Red Army, the armed forces of the Soviet Union, our Allies from the East, in the region of the River Elbe in Easter Germany. Armed conflict, however, was to continue in the Pacific region, against Japan, until the end of the year, when this final part of the world war came to an abrupt end after the devastating atom bomb attacks on Hiroshima and Nagasaki on mainland Japan.

The subsequent post-war years were a raw time for most European countries, in particular, and also for the UK. Rebuilding had to begin and food rationing continued for ten years, well into the 1950's. Construction materials were in short supply, and restrictions on the import of building timber lasted for a similar period of time, finally being de-controlled in about 1953–54. War damage repairs to homes affected by aerial bombardment was a significant imperative, and it took years to complete all that was outstanding. House building was urgent, especially for those whose homes had been flattened by air raids, and making good with all kinds of reconstruction proceeded as quickly as the circumstances could allow.

Service personnal returning to civilian life needed opportunities for employment. The education system had to make up for a lost generation of early and middle school learning that had been badly disrupted by school closures during the years of conflict – some sporadic and short term, some lengthy, depending on where you lived and the degree of interruption experienced – as there had been a shortage of teachers during the war, because many schoolmasters had to serve in the armed forces. Aspirants to teaching, recently vacating lengthy service in the war zone, and needed to fill the recruitment gap, had to be hastily trained and assigned.

In 1945 I had never really known peace-time, so I suppose there was a certain anti-climax from the dramas of war years; but a new future was opening up.

My thoughts had been that this comprehensive war was a final confrontation of good and evil to inaugurate peace and civilised living long term. We continue to benefit from years of peace in Europe, although the lesson still needs to be heeded by so many conflicts across the world today.